GHOSTS ON THE PENISTONE LINE

Featuring stories from Sheffield, Barnsley, Penistone, Huddersfield, & Beyond

Adrian Finney

Strange Britain

Copyright © 2023 Strange Britain

All rights reserved

No part of this book may be reproduced, or stored in a retrieval system, or transmitted in any form or by any means, electronic, mechanical, photocopying, recording, or otherwise, without express written permission of the publisher.

Text & Design copyright Adrian Finney 2023

www.strangebritain.uk

facebook.com/strangebritain

strangebritain.eventbrite.com

email: strangebritainofficial@gmail.com

Manuscript Edition 230820-D

This book covers the line as if ridden from Sheffield to Huddersfield.

However, the chapters can be read in any order, so if your journey begins at a different station, or travels from Huddersfield to Sheffield, please feel free to read the stories in the order you traverse the line.

CONTENTS

Title Page	
Copyright	
A Brief History of the Penistone Line	3
Sheffield	6
The Phantom Policeman	13
The Megatron	18
Meadowhall	22
Chapeltown	25
Elsecar	29
Wombwell	33
Lundhill Colliery	37
Barnsley	42
Barnsley District Hospital	46
Summer Lane	49
Dodworth	52
Silkstone Common	54
Penistone	59

Penistone's Corpse Candles	67
The Sharp Dressed Man	71
The Woodhead Tunnels	73
Brockholes	80
Denby Dale Viaduct	82
Denby Dale	84
Shepley	87
Stocksmoor	90
Honley	92
Robin Hood Tunnel	95
Berry Brow	98
Lockwood Viaduct	101
Lockwood	104
Huddersfield	108
Jackpot Mary	113
The Healing Ghost	115
Ghosts on the Lines	117
Special thanks to the Penistone Line Partnership	123

GHOSTS ON THE PENISTONE LINE

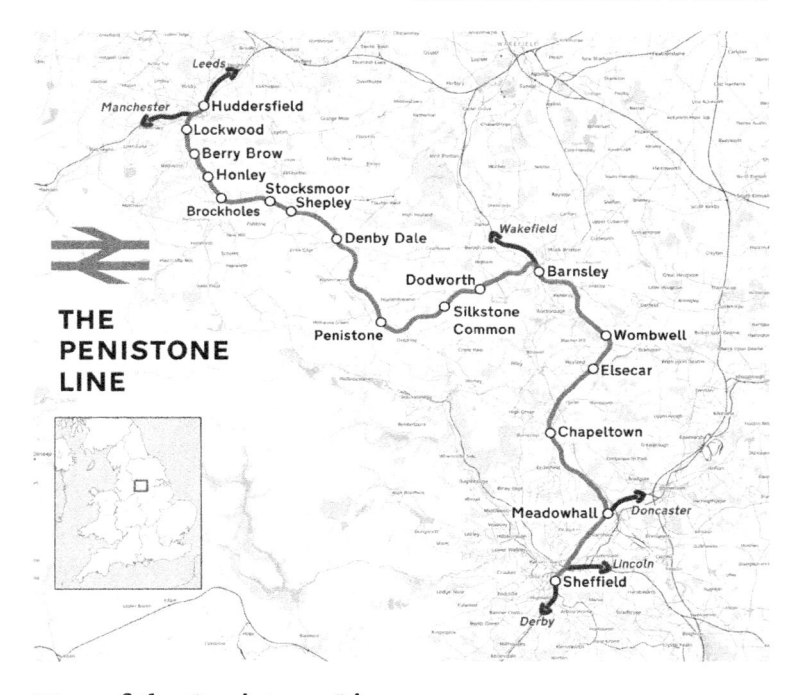

Map of the Penistone Line
(source: OpenStreetMaps)

1

A BRIEF HISTORY OF THE PENISTONE LINE

The Penistone Line is a 27-mile railway with 17 stations, running between Sheffield and Huddersfield. It played a vital role in transporting coal, textiles, and other goods from the industrial towns of West Yorkshire to Sheffield and beyond. The line was originally opened in stages by different railway companies, and was extended from Penistone to the former Sheffield Victoria Station by the South Yorkshire Railway in 1854. The line stayed in this configuration for the next century, until the South Yorkshire Railway was absorbed by the London, Midland, and Scottish Railway (LMS) in 1923, who took over the line.

In 1948, the Transport Act was passed, leading to the creation of British Railways. The "Big Four" companies were merged into a single entity, British Railways, which became responsible for the management and operation of the national rail network. British Railways introduced new locomotives and rolling stock, and the Penistone Line was modernised.

However, the line from Sheffield Victoria to Penistone was an early casualty of the Beeching Report, which was commissioned in 1963 to address financial losses and inefficiencies in the railway system. The report resulted in significant line closures, with thousands of miles of track and numerous stations shut down, including Sheffield's Victoria Station. The Penistone Line was one of the lines that survived the Beeching cuts, and it continued to operate under British Railways.

In 1994, the re-privatisation of British Rail began, leading to the fragmentation of the network into multiple train operating companies. The Penistone Line was operated by Regional Railways until the early 2000s, when Northern Rail took over the line.

Today, the Penistone Line is a popular commuter route, and it is also used by tourists who want to experience the beauty of the Yorkshire countryside. The line is home to more than its fair share of ghosts and hauntings, and it is said to be one of the most haunted railways in the UK.

GHOSTS ON THE PENISTONE LINE

SHEFFIELD

When Sheffield Midland Station opened back in 1870, it already had been the unlikely centre of a supposed ghostly riot, an incident that those present would much sooner we all forget.

Back in late 1868, rather fittingly on a full moon, residents living behind the station spotted a glowing figure darting unevenly out of their windows. The white figure was said to have terrified onlookers, so, within an hour of that first sighting, a frenzied mob had taken to the streets hunting for what they believed to be a ghost.

Over the next several hours the mob increased in

both size and rowdiness until it became nothing short of a riot. At its peak over 2,000 men charged around the area, burning pitchforks in hand, causing widespread destruction in their wake. By morning the area of the city immediately behind the train station was a scene of utter devastation, with a bill of £70,000 put on the damages caused, a figure that works out at almost £8,000,000 today.

All over a ghost sighting.

Only in this instance? There was no ghost.

One of the local newspapers had uncovered the truth. A young lad, reported as being "of weak intellect," or a child being a child as we might say today, had fallen into some highly reflective white paint. Fearing that he'd be in a lot of trouble were his parents to find out? He opted to slowly sneak his way home. Unfortunately for him his sneaky behaviour, coupled with the highly reflective paint that shone under the light of the full moon, meant that the boy was spotted and soon found himself chased by an angry mob believing him to be a ghost.

With the truth now out in the open? The city, rightly, was ashamed of its actions.

When the first goods trains began passing through the station in 1869, travelling along what's now the Midland Mainline, they brought something along with them. A character infamous in British folklore and one with a name that became forever linked to Sheffield:

Often said to be an impossibly tall man with burning red eyes, a long flowing cape, and a top hat, Spring Heeled Jack is a legendary figure who is said to have terrorised people across the United Kingdom in the 19th and 20th centuries. His most unusual aspect is his ability to jump impossibly huge distances and to climb seemingly unclimbable walls. He is often found peeping through windows before leaping across rooftops, letting out a maniacal cackling laugh.

Spring Heeled Jack was first spotted in 1840 in the Whitechapel area of London. By the end of that decade, sightings of him had spread across much of the UK. However, it wasn't until 1869 that Jack made his way to Sheffield. Sightings, matching those earlier ones in Whitechapel, were initially made around the Heeley area. The Midland Railway was coming to town, with Sheffield and Heeley stations both officially opening in early 1870, and it looked like Jack had come along for the ride.

The initial clutch of sightings were all on Chesterfield Road in an area centred around the railway bridge and the old Heeley Station. All the witnesses claimed that they'd seen a tall thin figure, with glowing red eyes, who leapt impossible distances as he bound across the rooftops.

By 1871, Jack had made his first appearance in Attercliffe. The sightings again matched those initial reports from Whitechapel back in the 1840s and from Heeley just a couple of years earlier. He was said to be banging on doors and windows, peering in, and then laughing maniacally as he jumped away across the rooftops.

By the 1880s, reports across the country were starting to wane. The last recorded sighting in Whitechapel, the place where Jack first thrust himself out on to the world, happened just a couple of days before another Jack was to appear on the scene. That other Jack? He was the infamous serial killer Jack the Ripper, who began his horrific murder spree on a Whitechapel already terrified by his Spring Heeled namesake, and would eventually become a name even more widely known and feared than Spring Heeled Jack ever had been.

Within a few years, Spring Heeled Jack was remembered as nothing more than an urban legend.

Many assumed that would be that for Spring Heeled Jack, but Sheffield hadn't yet seen the last of him.

In the early 1920s, the people of Attercliffe were woken by the sound of someone, or possibly something, racing across their rooftops. On groggily looking out of their windows, they saw a figure, one who perfectly fit the description of Spring Heeled Jack, jumping effortlessly from rooftops on one side of the street to rooftops on the other.

The residents, now suddenly very much awake, watched in fear as Jack leapt while his maniacal laughter filled the air.

The police were summoned, but aside from damage to the rooftops that would have been consistent with a heavy man running around on top of it, nothing more was found. After a half dozen more sightings over the next two weeks, Jack was once again gone.

Twenty years later, Sheffield found itself under a very different kind of attack. On December 12th 1940, the Sheffield Blitz took place. German bombers targeted the city's many steel works, killing almost 700 civilians, and leaving over 40,000 homeless.

In the midst of all this chaos, Spring Heeled Jack made a return. He was first spotted in Heeley, where he was running up and down the rooftops on Chesterfield Road, cackling his manic laugh, a laugh so loud that it rang out above the sounds of the falling bombs. He was also seen once again around Sheffield Station. As the platforms took damage from a direct hit, those on the scene reported seeing Jack's frame dancing amidst the flames, frolicking in the devastation.

By 1945, the sightings had again ceased, and many thought, once again, that was thankfully that.

However, Jack had other plans, with the most recent spate of sightings in the city saddling the late 1970s into the early 1980s.

The current station, including its grand frontage and concourse, dates from 1905. The original station was struggling to keep up with demand so it was extensively rebuilt. The original Platform 1 was located where Platform 5 is now and the building there, housing a coffee shop and the toilets, was the original station building.

A large canopy was also erected covering the entire station including all the tracks that provided cover from the elements. If you look closely you can still make out the mounting points for the iron framed structure.

During the Sheffield Blitz, Midland Station was extensively damaged. The station once had a curved, fully covered canopy roof covering the tracks, which would have made the platforms a much better place to wait during bad weather.

Sadly, this was destroyed in the bombings, leaving just the platform shelters that we have today. Interestingly, Bath Green Park station in the south of England still has an identical canopy that survives to this day. Train companies often reused designs and plans as a cost-cutting measure, so it's a curious visit to think how different the current station could have been had it survived.

In the early 2000s, a group of friends had just gotten off the last train in the station that night. As they looked up, something felt a bit off about the station. Before they knew it, they felt the ground shake around them, they heard bombs dropping, and they saw the roof collapse around them. Curiously, however, the falling roof vanished before it reached the ground, leaving the men deeply shaken by their experience.

It was almost as if they had witnessed the station's destruction, an event that occurred almost 60 years before their experience. But how could that have been?

THE PHANTOM POLICEMAN

The platforms of Sheffield station are also said to be the home of another seemingly out of place entity. Back in the late 1940s, when the station was going under a major renovation following the damage caused during the Sheffield Blitz, workmen kept spotting an odd looking policeman on the opposite platform.

He was described as being short, of a stocky build, and with huge "mutton chops" style ginger sideburns and a well kept moustache. His uniform also looked "off" to them too, almost like it was decades out of date. He'd be there, watching them, and then in the blink of an eye he was gone.

He was back again a few years later when, in the early morning hours of February 1953, a lone train conductor was making his rounds when he saw a figure standing on the platform, wearing a long black cloak and a distinctive looking police helmet. The figure had a handlebar moustache and large ginger mutton chops. The conductor thought it was strange to see someone out so early, especially a policeman, but at the time he didn't think much.

The next sighting occurred just a few days later, only this time it was in the middle of the day. A group of friends were waiting for their train when they saw the same figure standing on the edge of the platform opposite. They turned away, as they were all a little spooked, although they couldn't explain why, and when they turned back he was gone. Which, given it was just a few seconds that they had their gaze averted, should have been impossible. They didn't want to make a scene, so they just opted to keep quiet about their sighting, until they got back to Sheffield later that day.

A chance encounter with the conductor who had seen the figure just a few days earlier brought home the reality of their encounter to all involved.

In the early 1970s a group of football fans were at the station, awaiting the first train of the day, as they were travelling to see their beloved Sheffield United play away. It was still long before dawn yet the men were already in a rowdy mood when they spotted a police officer, on the platform opposite them, just staring at them.

It was almost like he was daring them to do something wrong and the men felt something was definitely off about him. His uniform, for one, just wasn't right. It looked like a museum piece. As they watched, their train pulled into the station so they got on board. As they took their seats they looked through the windows at the platform opposite the policeman was nowhere to be seen.

Late one evening in 2007, a young woman was waiting for her train at Sheffield train station. She was tired and stressed, and she was looking forward to getting home. As she was waiting, she saw the ghostly policeman standing on the platform. He hadn't been there just a second earlier and she had no idea where he'd appeared from.

She looked at him intently. He was short and round, with large ginger mutton chops and a handlebar moustache. His uniform looked like it had been taken from a museum exhibit and there was something odd about him as though he was there but somehow wasn't there.

She was startled, but she also felt a sense of calmness, which surprised her looking back. Rationally? She knew fear would have been a more appropriate response.

The policeman looked at her and smiled. *"Don't be afraid, lass"* he said. *"I'm here to help you."*

"Help me?" she replied with confusion. *"With what?"*

"With whatever you need, love," the policeman said.

"I'm here to watch over you, and this place, and protect you."

She smiled back at the man's moustached face. *"Thank you,"* she said. *"I think I need that."*

The man nodded. *"You're welcome,"* he said, smiling softly. *"Now, get thi'sen 'ome and get thee some rest."*

As she watched, transfixed, the policeman vanished into the evening. She felt a sense of peace and security that she hadn't felt in a long time. She knew that she would be okay, that it would all be okay, and took comfort from the fact that this phantom policeman was there to watch over her.

The most recent sighting occurred in 2020, in the early morning hours, when a night security guard saw a short, broad figure in a police uniform standing on the platform. The figure was once again described as having large ginger mutton chops, a handlebar moustache, and was wearing an old policeman's hat and cape. The security guard was startled, but the figure simply turned and walked away, vanishing into the thin air.

Sightings have occurred at all times of the day and night, and they've always been on the island that contains platforms 2 to 5, so could this be because that is the oldest part of the station?

No one knows who the phantom policeman is, or why he's chosen to haunt Sheffield train station. Some people believe that he is the spirit of a police officer who was tragically killed in the line of duty, whilst others believe that he may have died in an accident on the railways, and that the station was once part of his beat. With the surviving records of that era being incomplete? We're left with no other option other than to speculate.

This author likes to think that, whatever happened to him, he's chosen to become a guardian spirit, watching over the station and its passengers.

THE MEGATRON

Sheffield's Megatron, known officially as the River Sheaf Culvert, is an underground watercourse that runs beneath the city. Its history dates back to the 18th century, when Sheffield's industrial expansion led to the construction of a complex network of culverts and tunnels to accommodate the city's growing population and its increasing need for water management.

The Megatron itself was built in the mid-19th century as part of the city's efforts to control and divert the River Sheaf, which had been prone to flooding. This underground culvert, measuring approximately 1.5 miles in length, serves as a major storm drain, carrying excess water away from the city centre and preventing flooding in the surrounding areas.

The area around it was once marshland, but thanks to the Megatron being built, the land was made usable. Originally, the Megatron was constructed using brickwork and stone, showcasing the craftsmanship of the time, and it is a testament to its Victorian engineering that it still functions exactly as designed, and that it looks like it will continue to do so for centuries to come.

In recent years, the Megatron has gained a certain allure, attracting urban explorers and photographers who venture into its dark and mysterious depths to capture its stark beauty. Every summer The Porter Trust, who help manage the watercourse, operate guided tours down into the tunnels, and this is the only safe and legal way to experience the majesty of the Megatron.

The scale of the three main chambers of the

Megatron cannot be overstated. They're hundreds of metres long and have the height of several double-decker buses, making them huge chasms, almost like underground cathedrals. If you're on Platform 5 of Sheffield Station, you might notice a couple of wooden hatches on the platform, near the coffee shop. Were you to open one, you'd find one of the subterranean antechambers that lead towards the Megatron itself, hiding in plain sight.

There's said to be a lot of dark spirits down there. When the Romans were marching through the area, almost two millennia ago, they recorded that those living in what's now Sheffield believed that a water spirit or possibly even a water god lived beneath the city, and that it wanted offerings to appease it. The Romans were fearful of this spirit, as they saw how the locals revered and worshipped it, and it is because of this that they avoided the area.

The spirit has, on occasion, been reawakened. Most recently, during the redevelopment of Hartshead Square and the construction of The Star Building, back in the 1980s and 1990s. Two wells were uncovered by archaeologists and they realised that, whatever was down there, it had been highly venerated for they found offerings spanning around 1,200 years. Coins, valuable trinkets, and even sacrificial animal bones were taken for study and this seems to have angered the spirit. Construction on the area was plagued with mishaps and workers refused to be on the site alone for they felt they were being targeted by what they described as a "dark presence."

In recent years, the spirit appears to have returned to its slumber, but we must never forget that it's still there, underneath Sheffield, and that sooner or later it's likely to once again reawaken.

Perhaps you're also wondering where the name "Megatron" hails from? In truth, no one knows for sure, but one theory is that in the 1980s, when urban explorers found the huge structure, they nicknamed it after the leader of the Decepticons in the Transformers cartoon, as unlikely as that sounds.

MEADOWHALL

Meadowhall Interchange is by far the newest station on the Penistone line, having officially opened on September 4, 1990, to serve the new and neighbouring Meadowhall shopping centre, which opened on the same day. The station was built to replace the old Wincobank station, which had closed in 1953. The new station was designed by the architects John McAslan and Partners, and is built in a modern style incorporating both a bus station and a terminus for the city's trams.

Despite the current station being the young upstart on the line, it's far from the first station to be called Meadowhall. Back in 1855, a short distance from the current station, Wincobank and Meadow Hall Station opened its doors and was built by the South Yorkshire Railway. Somewhat confusingly, there was also a Meadow Hall and Wincobank Station located a short walk away in Tinsley. In 1868, after a decade of confusion, one station became Meadow Hall while the other became simply Wincobank.

Wincobank was located just before the line branches at Meadowhall Interchange, and supposedly nothing is left of the station at track level. However, there are those who have claimed to have glimpsed this long-gone station from on the tracks. Several freight train drivers, whose routes have taken them along that line during the early hours, and who have been forced to slow for a warning signal, all claim to have seen the long-demolished station as they pass through. Only it isn't quite there. It's almost like they're witnessing a memory of the station, or perhaps a manifestation, one that hasn't fully materialised, leaving a dark and unsettling feeling in the pit of their stomach.

Brightside Station, also in the vicinity, which closed in 1995, does still have its now-dilapidated platforms visible, and was put forward to the drivers as the possible cause of their sightings. The drivers were all deeply offended by this suggestion. As professionals, they knew their route, they knew where the former Brightside Station was, and they knew that they'd already passed through it when they had their sighting.

So is it possible that, by means as yet unknown, train drivers are somehow catching a glimpse back in time?

Back in August 1990, around a month before the station formally opened, workmen were putting the finishing touches to the station's lighting when they had an encounter that deeply unsettled them. As they stood along the platform, a young woman, in what to them appeared to be an old-fashioned dress, ran along the platform before leaping onto the tracks. Fearing the worst, the workmen hastily ran after her, but she was nowhere to be seen.

This happened several more times over the next few days and it was feared that the woman, whoever she was, was trying to commit suicide. On the eve of the station's opening, the woman was back, but this time it was evident that she wasn't trying to kill herself. She was actually something else entirely as she was translucent. The station's harsh lighting was shining through her form, giving her a washed-out and otherworldly complexion. Whatever she was? "Ghost" was the word that most readily sprang to mind.

A faded, translucent, ghost? This gave the station manager an idea. If he upped the lights' intensity by around 15%, it would be a subtle enough change so as not to dazzle the drivers of passing trains, but it would be enough extra light to wash out her ghostly form entirely.

Eventually, the station's lighting was altered as part of a 2006 rebuild, thus ensuring that there was always light on hand to wash out this ghost's unnerving appearances.

It's a unique approach to a repeated haunting, but it's one that, to date, appears to have worked for the ghost? She hasn't been seen since.

CHAPELTOWN

Chapeltown Station, an unmanned station in one of Sheffield's northern suburbs, opened in 1984. It was the first station opened by the then newly formed South Yorkshire Passenger Transport Executive. It replaced an older station, called Chapeltown South, that was located a very short walk up the line.

If you enter Chapeltown Station from Sussex Road you walk past the original station building and the remains of the surviving platforms of Chapeltown South.

It's hard to believe that this now unassuming commuter station once held an important place in

Britain's wartime effort.

Newton, Chambers, and Company were a prominent manufacturing company that was based in the area. Founded in 1866 by Thomas Newton and William Chambers, the company specialised in the production of fireproof safes, vaults, and other security products.

During World War II, Newton, Chambers, and Company played a crucial role in manufacturing fireproof storage cabinets for the protection of valuable records, such as government documents and historical archives. The work of their company saves countless irreplaceable artworks and priceless historical documents during the Blitz.

They also helped to manufacture and equip various other items in the war effort, including the Churchill Tank.

Their factory, located in Thorncliffe just outside of Chapeltown, had its own branch line leading up to it so that freight trains could roll straight up the the factory doors. Their line branched off just north of Chapeltown South and had its own station, Chapeltown Central.

In a typically Victorian manner Chapeltown South was located in the centre of Chapeltown, much as the current station that replaced it is, whereas Chapeltown Central wasn't technically located in Chapeltown at all. It was in neighbouring

Thorncliffe.

At some point in 1943 a train carrying freshly built tanks along with various munitions had left the Newton, Chambers, & Company factory, had safely passed through Chapeltown Central, and had joined the mainline. As it was passing through Chapeltown South Station, at around 9:15am, some explosives that were being carried in the train's rear carriage unexpectedly ignited, resulting in a huge explosion with devastating results.

Two soldiers were killed instantly who had been riding on the rear carriage, alongside a number of civilians who had been patiently waiting for their train on the northbound platform of the station.

Because the war was on, and with the belief that news of such an accident would be bad for public morale, the incident was quickly and quietly hushed up. No inquiry was ever held to ascertain what exactly caused the explosion, nor was the number of people killed on the platform ever officially confirmed. A look through Parish records suggest anywhere from 4 to 12 people might have lost their lives on that day, in addition to the two soldiers who were on the train's rear carriage..

In the years since the accident a number of people claim to have encountered the spirits of those who died that day. On certain days, typically around sunrise, they are said to hang around the old platforms that are still visible from the current station, only now they resemble living shadows rather than true human forms.

Some who have been lucky enough, or should that be unlucky enough, to have been entering the station from its Sussex Road entrance have had a particularly close encounter with the unsettled spirits.

To encounter them is to encounter a personification of loss itself, like being hit with a wave of pure grief and despair, making it an encounter that people are not quick to forget.

Perhaps if this incident, that occurred 80 years ago yet officially never took place, could somehow be formally acknowledged? Then perhaps the spirits finally be able to rest.

Or perhaps they are simply waiting for a train that, for their souls, is destined never to arrive?

ELSECAR

Before 1750, Elsecar was nothing more than a small hamlet set amidst beautiful farmland. However, all that was about to change, as rich coal seams were found deep beneath the village. In just a few generations, the village was left forever changed. As mining techniques improved, small workshops opened, making the tools needed for this trade.

Then in 1850, local landowner the 5th Earl of Fitzwilliam, who also owned the nearby Wentworth Woodhouse estate, decided that what Elsecar needed was centralised engineering works, and when his plans came to fruition it transformed the village into a manufacturing hub to be reckoned with.

However, the boom was soon over, but the plucky village of Elsecar was once again ready to adapt. Many of the surviving buildings were saved, and the successful Elsecar Heritage Centre, a living museum managed by Barnsley Museums Trust, opened in its place.

The Heritage Centre, housed within a beautifully restored historical building, attracts visitors from far and wide who come to explore its intriguing exhibits and learn about the village's past. It is also home to The Earl's Great Engine, the only Newcomen Atmospheric Engine still in its original location anywhere in the world, that was used to pump water out of the depths of the mines. The design was so revolutionary that it enabled miners to go deeper than ever before, and the engine was used continuously from 1795 until 1923 when it was finally replaced by electric pumps.

In 1973, in recognition of the engine's significance to the area and to the Industrial Revolution, it was declared an official scheduled ancient monument. A scheduled ancient monument is a nationally important archaeological site or historic building, given protection against unauthorised change. Scheduling is the oldest form of heritage protection in the UK, dating back to 1913. Scheduled monuments can be anything from prehistoric standing stones and burial mounds, through to the many types of mediaeval sites—castles, monasteries, abandoned farmsteads and villages—to the more recent results of human activity, such as collieries, and in this instance, The Earl's Great Engine.

To be scheduled, a site must be considered to be of national importance. This means that it must have significant archaeological or historical value, and it must be at risk of damage or destruction should protection not be granted. Scheduled monuments are protected by law, and it is illegal to carry out any work on them without a permit from the local planning authority.

There is a local legend of a ghostly figure that haunts the old buildings that now make up the Elsecar Heritage Centre. Legend has it that on moonlit nights, when the village is hushed and the streets are empty, a spectral woman, in a flowing white gown can be seen wandering through the Heritage Centre. Witnesses describe her as ethereal and graceful, but with a melancholic air surrounding her presence.

According to local lore, the ghostly lady is said to be the spirit of a woman who lived in Elsecar during the late Victorian era. Tragically, she was a victim of unrequited love, and her heartache was so profound that it is said to have tethered her soul to the place she once called home. Some variants of the tale say that the man she loved declined her advances, for he was already in love with another, whereas others believe that her lover was lost in an accident in the buildings that now make up the heritage centre.

Either way, visitors and staff members have reported hearing faint whispers and seeing fleeting glimpses of the apparition as she glides through the building. Some claim to have felt a chilling sensation or a sudden drop in temperature when in her presence. Perhaps she is searching for closure or perhaps still yearning for the love she lost.

WOMBWELL

Wombwell is one of the oldest towns on the line, dating back over 1,000 years, with its name deriving from Womba's Well, named after a local Viking chieftain.

Scrying is the art of gazing into a reflective surface, typically a mirror or water, with the intention of gaining spiritual insights or receiving information about the past, present, or future. It is believed to work by tapping into the subconscious mind, allowing images, symbols, or visions to arise, which can then be interpreted to provide guidance or understanding.

Scrying is an ancient technique found in various cultures throughout history. Of particular historical note is that the first documented practitioner who used a crystal ball, rather than water or a mirror, for scrying was Wombwell's own William Byg.

People came from far and wide to seek out William's services and advice and became something of a celebrity figure for his era. His specialty was finding lost items. One look into his crystal ball, and he would be able to advise people on where their lost items were, with an accuracy of almost 100%.

According to contemporary accounts, his crystal ball was not like the ones we imagine today. Before William found it, he had no powers. It was only when he found the ball, saying that it spoke to him, that he gained his scrying abilities.

It was said to be a stone, only very crudely round in shape, and it was a deep black in colour with a highly reflective surface. It also supposedly held "a magic over metal."

Another telling clue to its origins was that William claimed to have found it in a burning area of woodland, after seeing a light flash through the night sky. Could the ball have been a meteorite? Nickel-iron meteorites, whilst rare, would have had the properties of William's ball. The deep black, reflective surface and the clear magnetic properties.

Whatever its origins, it made him a popular man, whose skills where in high demand. The stone took him from the life of an impoverished beggar to one of relative luxury and with the outbreak of the War of the Roses, he found himself in more demand than ever before.

Agents from the rival factions, the House of York and the House of Lancaster, both sought William out, hoping that he could provide insight into the other side. Their hope was that he could see the future, and therefore offer a tactical advantage, and for this he'd be paid handsomely.

Being the proud Yorkshireman that he was, William opted to use his gift to benefit the House of York, and supposedly fed bad intelligence to their rivals. This decision helped spell the end for William, as he soon found himself under investigation by the church.

Eventually, he was charged with heresy, for proclaiming himself a false prophet, and for going against the teachings of the church. William pleaded guilty the charges and asked those conducting his trial for mercy.

No mercy was shown. We have this idea that those who were found guilty of heresy were burned at the stake, or faced some other horrible fate.

However, luckily for William, those severe sentences only became a thing almost a hundred years later, during the Reformation.

Given the severity of the charges, his punishment was rather mundane. He had his crystal ball confiscated, he had to promise never to dabble with the "dark and satanic" art of scrying again, and he had to confess his sins in a number of neighbouring towns and apologise.

After that, he went back to Wombwell and, within a few months, he was back to begging to survive. He supposedly lived in woodland behind where the train station now resides, and it is also believed that his crystal ball is still buried somewhere nearby.

That same woodland, Wombwell Woods, has a number of other ghost sightings associated with it. Some of those who have dared to walk through the woods at night claim to have encountered a figure said to resemble either a highwayman or Guy Fawkes. The shadowy figure steps out in front of people before promptly dissolving into nothing but thin air.

A lot of the paranormal activity is centred around a place locals refer to as Convict's Tunnel. It is a very short tunnel that passes under a former railway line and gained its name as it was used as a stopping point for prisoners being marched towards Leeds prison.

It is said to have a dark presence and an oppressive atmosphere in the air that instils despair and fits of hopelessness. Perhaps it should come as no surprise that the area of woodland surrounding the tunnel has sadly gained the unfortunate reputation of being a suicide hotspot, with the ghost of a particularly harrowing suicide said to haunt the area, terrifying all those unlucky enough to encounter it.

LUNDHILL COLLIERY

Lundhill Colliery was opened in 1836 by the Barnsley Coal Company. It was one of the largest collieries in the area, and it employed over 1,000 miners. The mine was a major source of coal for the local area, and it helped to fuel the Industrial Revolution. However, it was also the scene of one of the worst mining disasters in British history.

On the morning of 10 February 1857, a fire broke out in the mine. The fire was caused by a spark from a miner's lamp. The fire quickly spread through the mine, causing an explosion and a ceiling collapse, leaving the few miners who had survived the initial explosion trapped deep underground.

189 miners died in the disaster. They were all men, and they ranged in age from 15 to 60 years old. The bodies of the miners that were able to be recovered from the mine were buried in a mass grave in Barnsley.

The 1857 disaster at Lundhill Colliery was a tragedy. It was a reminder of the dangers of coal mining, and it showed the importance of safety in the mines. The disaster also led to changes in the way that mines were operated, and it helped to improve safety for miners.

Lundhill Colliery continued to operate for many years after the 1857 disaster. However, the mine began to decline in the late 20th century, and it closed in 1967. The site of the old mine is now a nature reserve.

The first reports of paranormal activity at Lundhill Colliery date back to the years immediately after the disaster. In 1858, a group of miners reported seeing the ghosts of their colleagues walking through the woods near the mine.

Since then, there have been reports of miners being seen walking around the site of the old mine, and there have been reports of hearing the sounds of men working underground.

One of the most well-known ghosts of Lundhill Colliery is the Candle Man. He is said to be the ghost of a miner who was killed in the 1857 disaster. The Candle Man is said to be seen carrying a candle in the darkness, and he is said to be a warning to miners to stay away from the dangerous mine shafts.

The first reported sighting of the Candle Man was in 1858, just a year after the disaster. A group of miners were working in the mine when they saw a figure carrying a candle in the distance. The figure was walking towards them, and the miners could see that it was a miner.

The miners were scared, but they decided to follow the figure. The figure led them to a mineshaft that had been sealed off after the disaster. The miners tried to open the mineshaft, but they couldn't. The figure then turned and walked away, disappearing into the darkness.

The miners reported the sighting to their supervisor, but he didn't believe them. He thought that the miners were just trying to scare each other. However, the miners insisted that they had seen the Candle Man, and they told their story to other miners.

Over the years, there have been many other reported sightings of the Candle Man. Some people have seen him walking through the woods near the mine, and others have seen him in the mineshafts. The Candle Man is always seen carrying a candle, and he is always seen alone.

In 1902, a group of children were playing in the woods near the mine when they saw the Candle Man. The children were scared, and they ran away.

In 1945, a miner was working in the mine when he saw the Candle Man. The miner said that the Candle Man was standing in the middle of the mineshaft, and that he was holding the candle up to his face.

In 1968, the mine closed down. A few years later, a group of teenagers were exploring the mine when they saw the Candle Man. The teenagers were scared, and they ran out of the mine.

Some people believe that the Candle Man is a warning to miners to stay away from the dangerous mine shafts. They say that the Candle Man is the spirit of a miner who was killed in the 1857 disaster, and that he is trying to prevent other miners from suffering the same fate.

The other well-known ghost of Lundhill Colliery is the Wailing Woman. She is said to be the ghost of a woman who lost her husband, her four sons, and her grandson in the 1857 disaster. Upon hearing the news of their deaths, she had a heart attack and died.

The Wailing Woman is said to be heard wailing in the night, and she is said to be a warning to women to stay away from the dangerous mine.

The first reported sighting of the Wailing Woman

was in 1858, just a year after the disaster. A group of women were walking through the woods near the mine when they heard a woman wailing in the distance. The women followed the sound, and they came to a clearing.

In the clearing, they saw a woman sitting on a rock. The woman was dressed in black, and she was wailing loudly. The women were scared, and they didn't know what to do.

The woman turned to the women, and they saw that her face was covered in tears. She said, *"My family is dead, and so am I. But we are not at rest."* And with that, she faded away into nothingness.

The women were so scared that they ran away. They didn't tell anyone about what they had seen, but the story soon spread, as stories often do.

Over the years, there have been many other reported sightings of the Wailing Woman. Some people have heard her wailing in the night, and others have seen her sitting on the rock in the clearing. The Wailing Woman is always seen dressed in black, and she is always seen wailing loudly.

It is clear that the effects of the 1857 disaster, and the death and destruction it caused, are still being felt to this day.

BARNSLEY

The station we now know as Barnsley Interchange originally opened in 1850 as Barnsley Exchange, although none of the original station remains. The current Interchange, which combines a bus station and a railway station, opened in 2007 and is by far the most modern-looking station on the Penistone Line. Travellers are able to change from bus to train and back all whilst undercover and protected from the elements.

There's a junction just to the north of the station where the Hallam Line, to Leeds, and the Penistone Line, to Huddersfield, diverge with Leeds trains continuing on northwards and Huddersfield trains veering off to the west.

In the late 1800s, the original Barnsley Exchange Station was a bustling hub of activity. Back then, the station was so busy that it was known for overcrowding, as the facilities could barely keep up with the demand. Trains came and went, carrying passengers and goods, as Barnsley was thriving.

However, there was a tale whispered among the station staff and locals about a spectral presence that they claimed haunted the old station building.

Legend had it that a young woman named Emily had been a regular passenger on the trains passing through Barnsley Exchange Station. It was on one such train that she met and fell deeply in love with a young man who worked at the station. The two of them hoped to elope and start a new life together.

As the story goes, Emily arrived at the station, anxiously waiting for her lover to appear, but he never showed up. Time passed, and despair consumed her. Believing she had been abandoned, Emily was overcome with grief and made a rash decision. She flung herself onto the tracks in front of an oncoming train, ending her life.

There was a cruel irony in her death: the train she'd thrown herself under was carrying the man she'd loved. He'd been delayed and was riding a later train. In an era before instant messaging, he had no way of letting poor Emily know he hadn't abandoned her; he was simply running late.

Grief overcame him, and he blamed himself for Emily's death. He opted to spend the rest of his life alone.

From the tragic night of Emily's death onwards, station staff and late-night travellers all claimed to have seen a ghostly figure resembling Emily wandering the platforms of the old station. She appeared as a forlorn spirit, dressed in a tattered Victorian gown, her eyes filled with sorrow and despair. On occasion, her ghost would have a more horrific visage, with the injuries that killed her clearly visible, shocking onlookers.

Witnesses reported hearing soft weeping and catching fleeting glimpses of her ghostly form, only for her to disappear into thin air. Some claimed to have felt a cold breeze or heard the sound of footsteps following them when no one was present.

Ever since the old station was demolished, there have been no more sightings of poor Emily. We can only hope that when the old station was demolished, her spirit was released and is finally at rest.

The town was also once home to Barnsley Court House Station, known by locals as High Station, with the surviving station known as Low Station, which was built in 1848 and closed in 1964. During the Victorian era, the station was said to be home to a number of ghosts.

One of the more unusual sightings from the station involved a young woman who was waiting for a train one night in the winter of 1850. The woman was wearing a white dress and she was carrying a small child. She was waiting on the platform when an unusual-looking train pulled into the station. The woman stepped onto the train, but the train did not leave. Instead, it disappeared into thin air, taking the woman and the child with it. They were never seen again.

There were 23 people on the platforms that evening who all reported seeing the unusual vanishing. Talk of the story carried on for decades after the incident before it finally faded away, becoming a forgotten memory.

Another ghost story associated with the former station involved a man who was working as a porter at the station in the early 1900s. The man was working late one night when he heard a noise coming from the waiting room. He went to investigate, and he saw a figure sitting in one of the chairs. The figure was a woman, and she was wearing a long black dress. The woman was crying, and she told the porter that she had lost her husband. The porter tried to comfort the woman, but she just disappeared, leaving behind nothing more than a faint smell of perfume.

There were also reports of people seeing a ghostly train on the tracks near the station. Some people believe that this is the same phantom train that the woman and child boarded back in 1850. They believe that the train is carrying the souls of the woman and child, along with other restless souls, towards some unknown final destination.

BARNSLEY DISTRICT HOSPITAL

Barnsley District Hospital was founded in 1876 as the Barnsley Union Infirmary. It was built on the site of a former poorhouse, and it was originally intended to provide healthcare to the poor and working class of Barnsley. The hospital was renamed Barnsley Municipal Hospital in 1930, and it was renamed St Helen's Hospital in 1935. In 1948, the hospital joined the newly formed National Health Service.

A major redevelopment of the hospital was completed in 1977, and the hospital was renamed Barnsley District General Hospital. In 2005, it was renamed again, this time to Barnsley Hospital.

The first reports of paranormal activity at Barnsley District Hospital date back to the early 1900s. In 1907, a nurse reported seeing the ghost of a young girl on the children's ward. The nurse described the girl as being about 10 years old, with long, dark hair and blue eyes. She said that the girl was wearing a white dress and that she was sitting on the edge of her bed.

One of the most well-known ghosts at Barnsley Hospital is a child known as Sally. Sally is said to have died in the hospital during the Spanish flu pandemic of 1919, and her ghost is said to haunt the ward where she died. Witnesses have reported seeing a young girl in a white dress walking down the corridors, and some have even claimed to have been touched by her.

Another ghost said to haunt Barnsley Hospital is a woman known as the Grey Lady. The Grey Lady is said to be the ghost of a former nurse who died in the hospital in the 1970s. She is said to appear in the corridors of the hospital, and some witnesses have claimed to have seen her sitting in a rocking chair in an empty office.

The sounds of children wailing have also been reported on the Infectious Diseases ward at Barnsley Hospital. These sounds are said to be the ghosts of children who died in the ward during the 19th century.

In addition to these individual ghosts, there are also reports of more general paranormal activity at Barnsley Hospital. Lights have been seen to flicker, doors have been known to open and close on their own, and footsteps have been heard in empty corridors.

The reasons for the hauntings at Barnsley Hospital are unknown. Some believe that because the hospital is built on the site of a former poorhouse, the ghosts of the poorhouse's inhabitants are still lingering. Others believe that the ghosts are simply the spirits of patients and staff who have died at the hospital.

Whatever the reason, it is clear that something paranormal is still haunting Barnsley Hospital to this day.

SUMMER LANE

Summer Lane railway station was a railway station on the Barnsley to Penistone line situated some 1 mile 16 chains from Barnsley Exchange. The station was opened in 1854 by the Manchester, Sheffield and Lincolnshire Railway and was closed between December 1859 and February 1867 when it was reopened. It was finally closed by British Railways on 29 June 1959.

The station was situated on the east side of Summer Lane, close to its junction with Barnsley Road. The station had two platforms, each with a single-storey brick building on the platform. The station was originally served by trains running between Sheffield and Penistone, but these services were withdrawn in 1959.

The station buildings were demolished in the early 1960s, and the site of the station is now occupied by a housing estate. It was the first station on the Barnsley to Penistone line to be opened.

The trackbed of the line through is still visible and there is a footbridge at the site of the former station.

Curiously, from 1928 until 1959, it was the only station in the country whose goods yard was reserved solely for jam.

There was a young woman named Alice who was working as a ticket collector at Summer Lane station in the early 1900s. She was a kind and gentle soul, and she was well-liked by the passengers, and she loved her job. She'd had to fight hard for her job, as the prevailing thought at the time was that working on the railways was no place for a woman, but she quickly proved herself more than capable.

One night, Sarah was working the late shift when she saw a man standing on the platform. The man was tall and thin, and he was wearing a long black coat. He had a pale face and his eyes were sunken and dark.

Sarah felt a sense of unease as she looked at the man. She tried to smile at him, but he just stared at her with cold, dead eyes.

The man then stepped onto the tracks, and Alice watched in horror as he was hit by a train. The train dragged the man's body along the tracks, and Sarah could hear his screams of pain as he was killed.

Sarah was traumatised by what she had seen, and she rushed down the tracks screaming, alerting the train crew to what had just happened.

Much to her surprise, especially given what she had witnessed, there was no evidence that anyone had been hit by the train. No body, no blood, nothing.

Alice contemplated quitting her job at the station shortly afterwards and went as far as handing in her notice. Her boss asked why and she told him about her experience, fully expecting ridicule, but instead she got offered a mug of gin and was told that her resignation was NOT acceptable.

Her boss explained that he, too, had seen that figure and it was a ghost. Or rather, as he explained it, it was an echo of an event that happened at the station back in the late 1850s.

An old gentleman who was riddled with cancer had used the oncoming train as a way to end his suffering.

A few nights later, Alice encountered the figure again, but this time she wasn't afraid. She walked up to him and went to place her arm on the ghost, telling him his suffering was over, and with that? The ghost softly smiled and vanished. The tormented spectre was never seen again.

DODWORTH

Dodworth station was opened in 1854 and was originally built as a single-platform station, but was later extended to two platforms in 1893. Dodworth station was closed to passengers in 1964, but remained open until 1985 for use by coal trains from the adjacent mine. When the mine closed, so did the station.

Then, in 1989, Dodworth got a reprieve. South Yorkshire Passenger Transport Executive invested in the Penistone line, recognising its importance in connecting remote communities, and the station was reopened.

The old signal box at Dodworth station was built in 1893, and it was once a hive of activity. Signals were constantly being switched, and trains were coming and going all day long. The neighbouring mine ensured that. But when the station closed to passengers in 1964, the signal box was abandoned.

Now, the old signal box is a somewhat lonely place. The only sounds are the wind whistling through the cracks in the walls, and the occasional train passing by on the tracks. But some say that the old signal box might not be as empty as it seems.

They say that the ghost of a young signalman still haunts it to this day. The signalman was killed in a train accident in 1959. At least, that's what the official inquiry stated. Curiously, his body was never found. He was said to have been napping in a wagon that was inadvertently hauled away to be filled with coal, and no one saw him again.

The ghost of the signalman is said to be a tall, thin man with a pale face and dark hair. He is always dressed in his signalman's uniform, and he often carries a lantern. Sometimes, those travelling down the line on late autumn evenings see a floating light around the old signal box.

Those on the neighbouring level crossing also look up and they're sure they can see the signalman sitting there, waiting, and watching.

SILKSTONE COMMON

> THIS MONUMENT WAS ERECTED
> BY THE PEOPLE OF SILKSTONE PARISH
> IN 1988,
> TO MARK THE 150TH ANNIVERSARY
> OF THE TRAGIC EVENT ON
> 4TH JULY 1838.
> WHEN 26 CHILDREN WERE DROWNED
> IN THE HUSKAR PIT CLOSE TO THIS PLACE.

Silkstone Common Station was officially opened on 1 November 1855. From the very beginning, the station served as a vital link for transporting coal from the nearby Silkstone Colliery. The demand for coal during the Industrial Revolution led to the expansion of mining operations in the area, making Silkstone Common Station a bustling hub for coal trains. The station was expanded in 1874 to keep up with demand.

One of the earliest horse-drawn railways in the country, the Silkstone Waggonway, ended roughly where the station is now. It was built to haul coal from Silkstone Colliery to meet with the Barnsley Canal. Parts of a tunnel built for the waggonway can be seen behind the platform.

As mining activities diminished in the latter half of the 20th century, Silkstone Common Station faced challenges. In 1959, it was closed due to dwindling passenger numbers.

Thankfully, that wasn't the end for the station. It was reopened in 1983, albeit with a single platform and the old station house converted into a private residence. Trains were once again calling at Silkstone Common.

In early 1984 a young couple who had been using the newly restored service to visit relatives were waiting impatiently for the last train back to Huddersfield. It was a chilly February night, lit by a full moon, and as they waited for their train, they heard faint cries of despair, as well as what sounded like muffled cries for help. They walked around and realised that the sounds were coming from behind the platforms, where the old waggonway was. As they watched, small shadowy figures appeared around them before vanishing in the blink of an eye.

When their train finally arrived, the couple hurriedly boarded, fearful, and told the conductor of their encounter. He nodded. He had worked the line back in the 1950s, and he too had experienced this. He had a theory about what was happening, and it tied to something he had first heard as a young lad growing up in the nearby village of Dodworth.

Legend has it that on certain moonlit nights, the spirits of long-lost miners who had died in a horrific accident would rise from their resting place, and haunt the abandoned tunnels in the area where Silkstone Common Station now resides.

It was on July 4th 1838 when tragedy struck..

Torrential rain had been pouring for several days, resulting in flash flooding on the surface, and leaving the drainage ditches overflowing. With nowhere else to go, this water began flooding deep into the mines, causing those in its depth to begin a panicked scramble for the mine's exit. Miners tried desperately to escape with their lives but for many, sadly, their escape efforts were in vain. By the end of the day 26 people had died down in the tunnels.

Shockingly, the oldest victim was only a boy who had just turned 17, while the youngest child killed was only 7. The vast majority of those who died were under 13. Both boys and girls had died in the disaster, robbing the village of a generation of its children, and its impact is still felt in the village to this day as there are now two memorials to those who died and services are carried out, in memory of the victims, on every anniversary.

The Initial inquest, held in the Red Lion Pub a week after the disaster, found no fault with the company nor with mining practices. Controversially? It blamed the children as they had been ordered to stay in place by an older miner, but understandably, they tried to flee the mine and the rapidly rising water. The incoming water broke through a flood door, designed to keep the water out, and washed the children deep into the mine.

Despite valiant rescue efforts, only four children were saved. The echoes of their final pleas still lingered in the mines before the rising water drowned both their bodies and their voices. Frustratingly those miners who did follow orders, and stayed in place, survived

The disaster caused an outrage across England and even came to the attention of newly crowned Queen Victoria. The law was changed, with The Mines Act of 1842 being passed, making it illegal for women and girls, as well as forbidding boys under the age of 10, from working underground in a mine. The disaster also eventually led to a whole raft of safety measures being implemented in mines across the country.

As the years passed, tales of strange occurrences

emerged from around Silkstone Common Station, which was located directly above the site of the disaster. Late-night travellers waiting for their train have reported hearing disembodied whispers, carried in the wind. Child sized shadows dance along the platform, seemingly detached from any physical presence, and the sound of distant pickaxes and the clattering of coal carts reverberate through the air, despite there being no mining activity for over half a century..

Local folklore attributes these phenomena to the trapped spirits of the children, forever bound to the tunnels they once worked in. Some believe they seek closure, searching for their lost comrades or longing for the sunlight they never saw again.

So, if you find yourself at Silkstone Common Station on a moonlit night, take a moment to listen to the whispers carried on the wind. Perhaps you'll catch a glimpse of the ethereal child miners, forever trapped between the worlds of the living and the dead, sharing their tale of woe from a time long past. But remember, it's not a journey for the faint of heart, for the spirits of Silkstone Common are spirits with whom an encounter can trigger a debilitating wave of grief.

PENISTONE

Penistone station was opened in 1854 by the Sheffield, Ashton-under-Lyne and Manchester Railway. The station was originally a single-platform station, but was later extended to two platforms in 1893.

The station building is a Grade II listed building. It was designed by the architect John Henry Chamberlain in the Italianate style. The building is made of red brick with stone dressings. It has a central clock tower and a two-storey frontage.

The station has two platforms, which are linked by

a footpath level crossing. There is a car park at the station, and there are bus stops nearby, along with Penistone's town centre.

It is also the station where the Woodhead Line branched off towards Manchester.

The Woodhead Line was a railway line in northern England that connected Sheffield and Manchester. The line was built in 1845 by the Sheffield, Ashton-under-Lyne and Manchester Railway. It was a key route for coal and passenger trains from the South Yorkshire coalfields to the industrial cities of Manchester and Liverpool.

The Woodhead Line was closed to passenger trains in 1981, but it remained open for freight traffic until 2001. The line was then closed completely, and the track was lifted.

It was considered a challenging route to build and operate. The line crossed the Pennines, and it included some of the steepest gradients in the British railway network. The line was also prone to landslides and other weather-related problems.

This meant that it was a popular route for steam enthusiasts. The line's steep gradients and challenging scenery made it a test for locomotives. When it was operational, it meant you could catch a train from Sheffield to Manchester significantly quicker than is possible today. The Beeching Cuts of the 1960s suggested closing the Hope Valley Line from Sheffield to Manchester and retaining the Woodhead Line; however, because of all the rural communities along the Hope Valley Line, that one was ultimately saved and The Woodhead Line was closed.

Because of this, Penistone was, for many years, a vitally important station. And it is also one of the few places in the country where you can go and see a ghost station for yourself. Penistone once had four platforms, with two being right at the beginning of the Woodhead Line, and you can still see the track beds and platforms to this day, but they have been reclaimed by nature and now form part of a wildflower reserve.

Those standing on the former platforms, on particularly still nights, are also said to faintly hear distant sounds of a steam train from along the line. It is an eerie place to stand, on a platform next to a station building, knowing the trains and the tracks themselves are now long since gone. But with those distant, ghostly, sounds, it feels like a spectral train could arrive at any second.

If there is any station in the country where you would expect to find a ghost train, surely it has to be Penistone. In the late 19th century, the town gained an unfortunate nickname:

The Graveyard of the Railways

The lines around Penistone were an accident black spot on Britain's railway network during the latter years of the 19th and early years of the 20th centuries. The main line through the town was the Woodhead route of the Manchester, Sheffield and Lincolnshire Railway between Sheffield Victoria and Manchester, London Road. The line was heavily graded (steep) with a summit some 400 yards inside the eastern portal of the Woodhead tunnel.

Back when George Stephenson, the father of the modern railways, was seeking permissions for the world's first intercity railway between Manchester and Liverpool that opened in 1830, he'd been asked about the dangers of cows straying onto the line and whether it would be awkward were a train to hit one.

His heavily accented reply?

"Oo, ay, very awkward. For the coo!"

It would be 15 years later, on October 6, 1845, when the train versus cow theory would be put to the test on the outskirts of Penistone. A train, travelling at speed, struck a cow that had been left on the line by a drover. The impact caused the locomotive and carriages to derail, and the cow was killed instantly. Such was the force of the accident that the cow was almost entirely cut in half.

Thankfully, none of the passengers suffered any injuries aside from some minor bruising, although the guard was more severely injured, breaking his leg.

The most serious accident at Penistone occurred on February 23, 1884, when a passenger train derailed at Bullhouse Bridge. The accident killed 24 people and severely injured a further 40. Amongst the dead was famed railway engineer Massey Bromley.

An inquest was held and the cause of the accident was found to be an axle failure on the hauling locomotive. The Inspector's report acknowledged that the accident "could not have been foreseen or prevented". It did however question, among other matters, the use of inside cranked axles, and the use of iron rather than steel for these important components. Axle failures due to metal fatigue in iron cast parts was an endemic problem across the rail network in the late 19th century.

In 1885, there was another fatal accident at Penistone, when a freight train collided with a passenger train at Barnsley Junction.

Two wagons from a coal train, heading back to Shireoaks colliery, derailed, causing the locomotive to apply its emergency brakes.

As this was happening, a special excursion train was passing by in the other direction, composed of 18 coaches all full of families heading for a day trip to Southport.

The derailed wagons from the coal train struck several of the passenger carriages, causing them to derail, and resulting in 47 people being seriously injured and 4 people losing their lives.

The crew of the passenger trains' quick actions in applying the emergency brakes prevented what could have been a far greater loss of life.

Once again, an axle failure, due to metal fatigue in an iron part, was found to be the cause of the accident.

In 1889, there was yet another fatal accident at Penistone, when a passenger train derailed at Huddersfield Junction. The train was full of football fans from Preston heading to London to watch the FA Cup Final.

As it was an extra service, added due to demand, a train typically used to haul freight was being used.

As the train emerged from the Woodhead Tunnel, on a steep gradient, its brakes couldn't slow the locomotive down. When it reached the points at the next signals, the train lurched forward, jumping the points, and it derailed.

Miraculously, only one person died in this incident, but dozens were left severely injured. Those severely injured were taken to the Wentworth Arms Hotel, whose billiards room had been hastily adapted into an operating theatre. Dozens of limbs were amputated, which could account for some of the hauntings seen in the hotel even to this day.

It's said that the ghosts of those taken to the Wentworth Arms Hotel haunt the building to this day as it's known for unexplained occurrences along with poltergeist activity.

There were a number of other fatal accidents at Penistone during this period. The reasons for the high number of accidents at Penistone are complex. However, some factors that may have contributed include the line's steep gradients and sharp curves, the poor quality of the materials used in trains' construction, leaving them prone to metal fatigue, and the use of rolling stock unsuitable to the line.

The accidents at Penistone had a significant impact both on the town and the railway industry in general. The accidents led to a loss of confidence in the railway, and there were calls for improvements to safety standards. This led to changes in the way the railway was operated, including the introduction of new safety procedures, the improvement of track and signalling, and the phasing out of iron and the introduction of steel.

PENISTONE'S CORPSE CANDLES

Saint John the Baptist's Church, a short distance from Penistone Station, is said to be home to a regular manifestation of the phenomenon known as corpse candles. These are inexplicable lights, often said to flicker like candles, and get their name from the fact that they manifest themselves as floating lights, seen above churchyards and graveyards, especially above the graves of recently deceased people. Some say they are the spirits of the dead, come back to earth to light their way to the afterlife, whereas the most commonly held belief is that they're an omen of impending death and tragedy.

They were first recorded as seen back in July 1793. A curate at St John's Church, heading home after a late night of bookkeeping, spotted a white glowing light rising up from one of the graves. It then danced around the graveyard before returning to the grave it had risen from.

The next day, the grave the light had risen from had to be opened for, sadly, a young boy had died. The curate knew that the lights he saw must have somehow been an omen portending to the impending death of the young boy.

There have been many other sightings of corpse candles at St. John's Church over the years. In 1805, a woman named Mary Smith was dying, and her family saw a strange light outside her window. The light was described as being yellow and flickering, and it was said to move around the room. Mary Smith died shortly after, and her family believed that the light they had seen was a corpse candle, foreshadowing her death.

In 1820, a group of people were walking by the churchyard late at night when they saw a strange light floating above one of the graves. The light was white and flickering, and it seemed to be moving slowly towards the church. The group watched in amazement as the light disappeared into the church.

The next day, they were excited to tell their friends of their encounter when they heard some shocking news. There had been a fire in the village the night before and it had claimed 6 lives. Realising that what they'd seen wasn't a will-o'-the-wisp at all, but instead a corpse candle, they thought back on their sighting and shivered.

Another sighting occurred in 1846, when a group of people saw a corpse candle hovering over the grave of a young woman who had recently died. This corpse candle was said to have followed the group of people as they walked away from the grave, before disappearing into the night.

Whether you believe in corpse candles or not, there is no doubt that they are a fascinating phenomenon. These mysterious lights have been seen for centuries, and they continue to capture the imaginations of people all over the world.

One of the more infamous stories of corpse candles at St. John's Church is the story of the death of William Shaw. Shaw was a local farmer who died in 1854. On the night after his funeral, a group of people saw a light hovering over his grave. The light was said to be so bright that it could be seen from several miles away.

The next day, Shaw's body was exhumed, as the light had caused much anxiety around the village. It was discovered that he had died of a heart attack, but it was also clear that he had been accidentally buried alive. There were marks on his hands that showed he had been trying to claw himself out of his coffin.

The doctors who examined his body said that he had died so suddenly that he had not even had time to close his eyes. His death, or rather the true cause of his death, was understandably hushed up. But had the corpse candle not been spotted, the truth might never have been known.

The people who saw the corpse candle at Shaw's grave believe that it was a sign of his death. They say that the light was so bright because it was the soul of Shaw trying to say goodbye to the world.

In 1860, a woman was walking home from work when she saw a corpse candle floating above her own grave. The woman was so frightened that she ran home and didn't go out at night again for a week. Several weeks later, she received a letter. Her husband, who had been serving with the army at the time, had died during an incident at his training barracks. His death occurred on the night she saw the corpse candle.

In another sighting from 1860, a man named John Brown saw a corpse candle outside the church on the night of his father's death, his father having died unexpectedly of a heart attack.

In July 1884, a group of children were playing in the churchyard when they saw almost two dozen corpse candles floating around the graves. The children were so scared that they ran home and told their parents, who refused to let them go back to the churchyard ever again. Tragedy did indeed strike a couple of miles outside of the village, when a train crashed killing 19 people.

Sightings have continued right up to the present day.

THE SHARP DRESSED MAN

In the shadows of Cannon Hall, a peculiar phenomenon has been witnessed by locals and visitors alike. Reports of a sharply-dressed man, whose ghostly presence vanishes upon approach, have surfaced, sparking speculation as to the entity's back story.

Dating back to the nineteenth century, the apparition has been haunting the grounds surrounding the Deer Shed, leaving witnesses both mystified and unsettled. According to local folklore, this mysterious figure is believed to be the ghost of a young man with a tragic love story that echoes through time.

Legend has it that the man, a resident of Penistone, had fallen passionately in love with a family maid. Wishing to elope together and escape the judgmental eyes of their community, the star-crossed lovers arranged a clandestine rendezvous. Sadly, however, fate had different plans in store for them.

Before they could escape, their plan was thwarted, the young woman was forbidden from ever seeing him again, shattering the young man's dreams. In the face of this adversity, he made a heart-wrenching decision, and chose to join the army.

Tragically, his life was cut short, and he never had the chance to see his beloved again.

Inexplicably drawn to the place where his dreams of escape were shattered, the ghost of the sharply-dressed man returned to the Deer Shed, seeking the reunion that fate had cruelly denied him in life. Witnesses have attested to glimpsing this ethereal figure, dressed in a fashion reminiscent of the 1820s, drifting through the grounds of Cannon Hall.

However, as if bound by the rules of another realm, the ghostly figure vanishes into thin air whenever approached, leaving no trace of its presence.

Interestingly, Cannon Hall has an intriguing connection to the legendary Little John's bow. In 1729, the historic hall welcomed the bow's arrival after it was removed from Hathersage church.

THE WOODHEAD TUNNELS

A few miles to the west of Penistone are the Woodhead Tunnels. They were feats of engineering for their day and have been a magnet for ghost hunters since their closure.

In 1837, when work began on Woodhead, it was one of the most ambitious tunnelling projects ever carried out. Initially designed by Charles Vignoles, a highly respected engineer, the project was completed under the watch of Joseph Locke.

The project was plagued with problems and, upon its completion in 1845, it came in over double its initial budget. The human cost, however, was arguably even higher. Over 30 people lost their lives, another 200 people suffered injuries so severe they were left permanently "maimed" and unable to work again, and a further 500 people suffered broken limbs or other such injuries.

It was, however, a technical marvel being the first tunnel created under the Pennines. It bored through some of the toughest rocks in the country, was over 3 miles long, and given that they began boring from each end to meet in the middle, they were less than a third of an inch out in their margin of error.

There was another problem: the tunnel couldn't possibly hope to keep up with demand. Because of this, a second tunnel was built alongside the first and opened in 1852. The amount of deaths and injuries that occurred during the construction of Woodhead 1 would have a profound impact on the safety standards used during the construction of Woodhead 2, and as a result, no workers were killed during its construction due to accidents.

However, that's not to say that Woodhead 2 didn't have a human cost, because it most certainly did.

In 1849, shortly after construction began, a cholera outbreak hit the camp that housed the construction works and this resulted in 28 deaths.

Both tunnels were exceptionally busy, at their peak 500 trains passing through them every day. However, they quickly earned a reputation amongst train crews as the "Woodhead Hell-Holes." Because they were narrow tunnels with poor ventilation, the steam and smoke from the trains would linger, making them claustrophobic and dirty places to pass through.

There was a rumour that the lack of ventilation shafts, particularly in Woodhead 1, could cause train crews to pass out due to lack of oxygen. This rumour has a basis in reality. Both exits of the tunnel had exceptionally long sidings that trains, whose crews had been overcome by the smoke, could be diverted down where they could be allowed to come to a safe stop.

For years, a better solution was sought until finally, at the end of the 1940s, work began on a third tunnel, unimaginatively titled Woodhead 3. This was built to address the issues with the other two tunnels. The main issue being that Woodheads 1 and 2 were built decades before anyone had dreamt of an electric train, and when electrification was being mooted, they weren't wide or tall enough for it.

When Woodhead 3 opened in 1954, it was a huge tunnel, built to modern standards. It stood almost 8 metres high and almost double that in width, and it was also significantly longer than Woodheads 1 and 2. It was designed and engineered to last for centuries.

However, the world works in a funny way, and within a decade it already faced closure due to cutbacks across the rail network. One proposal, set forth in the early 1960s, would have seen the tunnel adapted and used as a motorway tunnel. When work began on Manchester's short M67 motorway, the initial proposals were for the road to be extended across the Pennines via Woodhead 3.

With Woodhead 3's opening, Woodheads 1 and 2 were passed to National Grid to be used to carry utility cables. In 1981, when Woodhead 3 closed to trains less than three decades after it opened, it too was taken over by National Grid.

In the decades since, there have been countless proposals to reopen the Woodhead Tunnels, but sadly it appears that it's something that will never happen. Woodhead 1 is considered in a poor condition, beyond repair, and is inaccessible on safety grounds. From the early 1960s, Woodhead 2 was used to carry high-voltage cables for National Grid until 2012, when, despite a massive backlash, the cables were transferred over to Woodhead 3.

From the 1980s up until the mid-2000s, it was actually possible to walk some of the Woodhead tunnels, and the tunnels gained a reputation as being haunted. Those brave enough to attempt the over 3-mile trek through them, with only torches for illumination, often heard voices and saw shadowy figures ahead, figures that appeared to flee from the torchlight, cowering and whimpering.

One such ghost hunter, let's call him John, had heard stories about the Woodhead Tunnels being haunted for years. John was a sceptic, but he was also curious. He decided to go to the tunnels and see for himself if the stories were true.

John arrived at the tunnels late at night. The tunnels were dark and silent. John could hear the wind whistling through them, so he took a deep breath and stepped inside.

John walked slowly through the tunnels, careful not to make any noise. He didn't want to disturb any ghosts or anyone else for that matter. What if there was someone else, exploring like him but from the other side? He didn't want to inadvertently make himself the ghost in someone else's story.

He walked for a long time, but he didn't see or hear anything. He was starting to think that he was right: the stories were just legends.

Just when John was about to give up, he heard a

noise. It was a faint sound, like someone crying. John followed the sound. It led him to a small chamber to the side of the tunnel, he estimated about halfway along, it was one of the tunnel's ventilation shafts.

In the chamber, John saw a figure. The figure was a man, and he was sitting on the ground. The man was crying. John could see that the man was hurt. He had a bloody wound on his head.

John approached the man and asked him what was wrong and if he could help. The man laughed and told John, rather matter-of-factly, *"It's too late for help now, lad, far too late."* With that, he promptly vanished into thin air, leaving only the sounds of his crying behind.

John was shocked. He didn't know what to say. He just stood there, listening to the man's faint cries until even they had faded away, leaving only a silence that hung heavy in the air.

John was left alone in the chamber. He didn't know what to think. Had he just met the ghost of a dead worker?

John left the tunnels and went home. He thought about what had happened for a long time. He didn't know if he believed in ghosts, but he knew that he had experienced something strange that night, and he knew what he saw.

John never went back to the Woodhead Tunnels, but he never forgot the ghost of the worker, and he often wondered what had happened to the man, and why he had been so sad. He didn't tell anyone his story for decades until, upon hearing of the Ghost Train project with the Penistone Line Partnership, he reached out to this author.

A great many of us experience things that we can't easily explain. We often sit on these encounters, unwilling to tell anyone, for fear of disbelief or ridicule. They can sit uneasy within us for years.

But in sharing those stories, for some, it offers release. The knowledge that their "secret" is now finally out in the open. And in many cases, those sharing their stories are simultaneously shocked, and relieved, to find out that a great many others have experienced the same thing as them. It proves that it must have happened. That can provide closure to many, although it also poses much larger questions about the nature of life and the afterlife.

BROCKHOLES

Brockholes railway station serves the village of Brockholes near Huddersfield in West Yorkshire, England. The station is 4.25 miles from Huddersfield on the Penistone Line operated by Northern Trains. Trains passing between Brockholes and Shepley pass through a 1-mile tunnel under Thurstonland.

The station was opened in July 1850 by the Huddersfield & Sheffield Junction Railway (a satellite company of the Lancashire & Yorkshire Railway), the station was formerly the junction for the Holmfirth Branch Line, which opened on the same day as the main line but closed to passenger trains on 2 November 1959 and to goods traffic in May 1965. Goods traffic ceased to be handled at Brockholes in October 1964, with the station becoming an unstaffed halt in August 1966. The southbound platform went out of use when the Stocksmoor to Huddersfield section was reduced to a single track in 1989.

The village is normally a quiet place, but on the night of October 14, 1982, it was the scene of a strange and unexplained event.

At around 10:30 PM, four people were sitting in a car in the village when they saw a bright light in the sky. The light was moving quickly, and it was about the size of a car.

The witnesses watched the light for a few minutes, and then it disappeared. After the light was gone, the witnesses felt an odd static feeling.

The four witnesses reported the incident to the police, but there was no explanation for what they had seen. The police investigated the area, but they found no evidence of a UFO.

The witnesses were all credible people, and they were all adamant about what they had seen. However, without any physical evidence, there was no way to prove that they had seen a UFO.

The Brockholes UFO sighting remains a mystery to this day. Some people believe that the witnesses saw a real UFO, while others believe that they saw something else, such as a meteor or a military aircraft, that might explain their sighting.

DENBY DALE VIADUCT

The Huddersfield and Sheffield Junction Railway was opened in 1850. The original plan was to build all of the viaducts on the line using stone, but due to a stonemasons strike, the viaduct at Denby Dale was hastily constructed using wood.

The first timber viaduct collapsed in a gale in 1847 before a single train had ever passed along it so was hastily replaced by a second timber viaduct. However, this viaduct was also found to be unsafe, and was eventually replaced by a stone viaduct in

1880.

The stone viaduct was designed by John Hawkshaw, and is 112 feet high and 15 chains long. It consists of 21 arches, each with a span of 40 feet. The viaduct was built by a local firm, Naylors, who tendered a cost of £27,650 and estimated a construction time of two and a half years. The viaduct was completed early, but at a significant loss to the contractors, as inexplicably they were fined for completing the project early.

The viaduct is 150 yards south of Denby Dale railway station, and is a grade II listed structure.

DENBY DALE

Denby Dale station was officially opened on 1 July 1850 by the Huddersfield and Sheffield Junction Railway. It was initially served by trains running between Huddersfield and Penistone.

In 1871, the station underwent significant renovations and improvements. A new station building was constructed, and the platforms were extended to accommodate longer trains.

The station is located near the famous Denby Dale Viaduct, an impressive structure spanning the River Dearne. The viaduct was constructed in the mid-19th century as part of the Penistone Line and remains a notable landmark in the area.

The station has been involved in various artistic projects. In 2001, a mural depicting scenes from the village's history was unveiled at the station. Additionally, the station and its surroundings have been a subject of interest for local photographers and artists.

The village of Denby Dale is known as "The Village of Pies" for its annual "Pie Celebration," a tradition that sees the village baking enormous pies to celebrate various milestones. In 1964, during the celebration of Denby Dale's 700th anniversary, a giant pie was baked and transported by train to London. Denby Dale station played a part in this unique event.

In July 1919, a couple who had been reunited after the Great War were standing on the platform of Denby Dale Station when they heard a train approaching rapidly from the direction of Huddersfield. It was late in the evening, and the young soldier assumed it must be a goods train, as he had disembarked from the last scheduled service of the evening.

Within seconds, they heard the train roar past, the couple felt the push of air displacement, and they smelt the coal. What they didn't see was the train itself.

The train felt so close that they could almost touch it, they certainly could hear and smell it, and they could even taste the acrid smoke it must have been bellowing out. Only their eyes had a clear view towards the tracks, and there was no train.

About thirty seconds after their encounter, they heard an almighty crash, of metal striking metal, and of people crying out in pain and in fear.

The young couple, realising that what they had

encountered was most likely otherworldly in origin, rapidly left the platform seeking somewhere safer to continue their reunion embrace.

Over the following century, others have also heard and felt this ghostly train race by, all terrified by the disconnect in their senses. Hearing, feeling, and smelling something that they just can't see.

Perhaps it's the ghost of an express train that derailed on 16 July 1884. The train had just passed through Denby Dale on its way to Manchester, via the Woodhead Tunnels, when tragedy struck. The locomotive's crank axle broke, causing the train to derail. The accident claimed the lives of 19 people and dozens more were injured.

And could the corpse candles, seen by the children in Saint John's Church, Penistone, have been an omen of this disaster?

SHEPLEY

Shepley station, which serves both Shepley and the neighbouring village of Shelley, was opened in 1850 by the Sheffield, Ashton-under-Lyne and Manchester Railway.

It has two platforms, which unusually aren't facing each other, instead they are staggered, with one on either side of a small road bridge that crosses the station.

The village of Shepley has been home to a carriage of a different kind since at least the mid-18th century. On only the coldest of winter's nights, between 2 and 4 a.m., a carriage drawn by four unnaturally large horses races around the village at a death-defying speed. However, given that this carriage can appear and vanish at will, and even when seen it is said to appear transparent, as though it hasn't fully manifested, perhaps those inside the carriage didn't defy death after all. Perhaps they died in an accident and their souls, still trapped in an echo of their carriage, have been fleeing their ghostly fate ever since.

The first known report of the carriage was back in 1752. A group of villagers were walking home from a night drinking in Shelley when they saw the carriage speeding down the road. They said that the carriage was filled with people, all of whom were dressed in black. The carriage disappeared around a bend in the road, and the villagers never saw it again.

There have been several other reports of the carriage over the years. In 1800, a man was walking home from work when he saw the carriage. He said that the carriage was so close that he could see the faces of the people inside. The people were all pale and expressionless, and they seemed to be staring right through him. He felt frozen in fear, unable to avert his gaze.

In 1900, a group of children were playing in the woods when they saw the carriage. They said that the carriage was coming towards them, and they were so scared that they ran away. They didn't stop running until they were safe at home.

The carriage has never been caught or identified. Some people believe that it is a ghost carriage, and that the people inside are the souls of those who have died in an accident, the details of which are now lost to history. Of course, there are others who believe that the carriage is a hoax, perpetrated by wealthy landowners, at the expense of those they see as beneath them.

At 3:30 p.m. on November 6, 2011, there was another sighting of something weird in Shepley. Unbelievably, several local residents all claimed to have seen a lioness walking with her cub down by the train station. As a direct result of this, trains were suspended on the Penistone line for the remainder of the day, and the police were called in. Those making the sightings were all absolutely certain in what they had seen.

Twelve police cars, a police helicopter, and several wildlife specialists all spent six hours searching for the mysterious lions, but alas, no evidence of their existence was ever found.

The surrounding area has a history of ABC, Alien Big Cat, sightings that date back in the 1990s. In 2005 a newspaper in nearby Meltham offered a reward of £500 to anyone who could get a photo of the large cat people had been seeing in the area.

STOCKSMOOR

Stocksmoor is a historic village with evidence of human occupation dating back to the Bronze Age. The village was mentioned in the Domesday Book of 1086 and was once a thriving market town. However, the village's importance declined in the 18th century, as the focus of trade shifted to larger towns with the onset of the Industrial Revolution.

Today, Stocksmoor is a quiet and peaceful village. The village has a number of historical buildings, including Stocksmoor Hall, which was built in the

17th century.

Stocksmoor station is 6.25 miles from Huddersfield on the Penistone Line. Most of the Penistone Line is single track between Huddersfield and Barnsley (and has been since 1989). However, Stocksmoor marks the first point (for Sheffield-bound trains) or last point (for Huddersfield-bound trains) where there is dual running track (the passing loop extends as far south as the next station at Shepley and most trains are scheduled to pass each other on this section).

The station was opened on 1 July 1850 by the Sheffield, Barnsley and Midland Railway. The station was originally called Stocksmoor and Brockholes, but the name was shortened to Stocksmoor in 1964.

Stocksmoor is a popular destination for walkers and hikers. The village is surrounded by hills and moorland, and there are a number of footpaths and trails in the area.

Stocksmoor is unique among the towns and villages along the Penistone line, as it's the one place that doesn't have any well-known ghostly legends. Given the village's long history this is quite surprising.

Now, that's not to say the village isn't haunted, it's just that if it is, people have kept quiet about their encounters.

HONLEY

The village of Honley, served by Honley railway station, lies approximately 3 miles south from Huddersfield. The station was opened by the Huddersfield & Sheffield Junction Railway (a constituent company of the Lancashire & Yorkshire Railway) in 1850.

The station was originally named "Honley Junction" as it was the junction of the Huddersfield & Sheffield Junction Railway and the Penistone Railway. The Penistone Railway was opened in 1851, and the two lines were joined by a bridge over the River Holme in 1852.

The station was renamed "Honley" in 1924. It was closed for goods traffic in 1964, but remained open for passenger traffic.

The village of Honley was once believed to be the home of an entity called Peggy o'th Lanthorn, which was said to be a Will-o'-the-wisp style manifestation.

Will-o'-the-wisps, also known as "ignis fatuus" (Latin for "foolish fire"), are mysterious and eerie natural phenomena that often appear at night. They appear as faint, flickering lights that seem to dance or float above the ground, luring travellers off their path.

They are often associated with spirits, fairies, or mischievous entities, and stories warn people against following the lights, as they could lead them to dangerous or haunted places.

Peggy o'th Lanthorn manifested as a playful light in the distance, but locals believed it to be a trickster spirit called Peggy. The origins of this belief are lost to time, but date back well into the mediaeval era.

Children were said to be at particular risk of being enticed by the lights. Soft, friendly singing was often heard alongside the lights, and the voice was said to be female and motherly in its tone, which could go some way to explaining how Peggy got her name.

Those children who followed her, however, were said to never be seen again. They had been lured away into a trap.

We now think of Tinkerbell, and other friendly-faced fairies, when we think of the Fae. However, if we look into the country's folklore, it is clear to see that the Fae were often seen as a much more malicious force.

They were often said to lure in children only for the children to never be seen again. Certain areas were considered gateways between our world and the world of the Fae, and it was believed that time passed differently there, so a few minutes in the fairy world could be decades here in our world, or even vice versa. Missing times and repeat abductions are also common themes in tales of the Fae.

It is surprising how much historic Fae legends have in common with the claims made by modern UFO abductees.

Widespread belief in the Fae folk never really established itself across Yorkshire. Perhaps this was due to the influence that the Vikings had on the county, or perhaps it was simply because the Fae themselves never established themselves here, apart from a few areas like Honley, where they are still remembered to this day.

ROBIN HOOD TUNNEL

Robin Hood Tunnel is 228 yards long, making it the shortest tunnel on the Penistone Line. It is situated in the village of Berry Brow. The tunnel was built between 1848 and 1849 by the Huddersfield and Sheffield Junction Railway (H&SJ).

The tunnel is a single-track tunnel, and is used by trains running between Sheffield and Penistone.

The tunnel is lined with brickwork, and the roof is supported by a series of cast iron beams.

The tunnel was opened to traffic in 1849. It was originally named Berry Brow Tunnel, but was renamed Robin Hood Tunnel in 1945, after the legendary outlaw Robin Hood, who is said to have lived in the area. The tunnel is also said to be haunted by the ghost of Robin Hood.

Sure. The legend of Robin Hood's ghost in Robin Hood Tunnel is a popular one in the area. It is said that the ghost of the legendary outlaw can sometimes be seen walking through the tunnel, or standing on the tracks.

There have been several reports of people seeing the ghost of Robin Hood in the tunnel. In one report, a group of children were walking through the tunnel when they saw a figure standing on the tracks. The figure was tall and thin, and it was wearing a green tunic and a hood. The children said that the figure disappeared as soon as they looked away, scaring them. Thankfully, for them, seeing the figure when they did meant that they'd left the tunnel before the next train passed through.

Railway lines, and especially railway tunnels, are no place for children to be playing.

In another report, a train driver was passing through the tunnel when he saw a figure standing in the middle of the tracks. The driver said that the figure was wearing a longbow and arrows, and it had a beard. The driver said that the figure disappeared as soon as he sounded the train's whistle.

Several other train drivers all claimed to have had similar encounters and the legend grew so much the tunnel was renamed in Robin Hood's honour.

BERRY BROW

Berry Brow is a village about 2 miles south of Huddersfield. It is one of the oldest villages on the line, having first been mentioned in the Domesday Book in 1086. Its unusual name is thought to come from the Old English words "beorh" meaning "hill" and "broc" meaning "stream".

Berry Brow was once a thriving mill village, at the heart of the Industrial Revolution, but the village's mills are now long gone.

The current Berry Brow station was opened on 9

October 1989, replacing the original Berry Brow station, which was located 300 metres to the north. The present station has a single platform and is unstaffed. Step-free access is available via a steep ramp.

The station is located close to the Deadmanstone, an ominously named natural rock formation that features a prominent hole running through it. The hole is large enough for a slim adult or child to crawl through.

The stone is about 10 feet tall and 6 feet wide, with the hole in the stone measuring around 4 feet long and 2 feet wide. The stone is made of sandstone.

The name "Deadmanstone" is thought to come from the fact that it was once used as a resting place for coffins on their way to burial. In mediaeval times, the church at Almondbury served as the parish church for the whole of the Holme Valley, and coffins from all over the valley would be carried there for burial. The journey to Almondbury was long and arduous, and it is thought that coffins were rested on Deadmanstone to give the bearers a break.

There is a local legend which states that the hole in the stone was used as a portal to the Otherworld. Bodies were said to be removed from their coffins, carefully passed through the hole in the Deadmanstone, and then returned to their coffins. The belief at the time was that by passing the bodies through the stone, their souls were able to pass over to the other side, leaving their bodies behind for burial or cremation.

There is also a claim that the stone was the site of the burial of a Viking chief or warrior.

Another local legend tells of a Roman soldier who was found walled up, having been bricked into either the small hole that runs through Deadmanstone or elsewhere in the grounds of Deadmanstone House. Deadmanstone House was a fortified manor house that was built around the stone some 1,800 years ago and of which nothing survives today.

The legend states that the soldier was found wearing full Roman armour, and that his bones were still intact. Some versions of the story say that the soldier was killed in battle, while others say that he was sacrificed to a pagan god. A further version claims that when unbricked, the soldier woke up, unharmed, and walked away, out into the night.

All legends are built upon a kernel of truth. With the Deadmanstone predating recorded history itself, we are left to wonder just what that truth might be.

LOCKWOOD VIADUCT

Lockwood Viaduct is a stone railway bridge that carries the Huddersfield to Penistone Line across the River Holme, in West Yorkshire, England.

One journalist, writing at the time of the bridge's completion, described it as *"One of the most stupendous structures of ancient or modern times."*

The viaduct was built between 1846 and 1848 by the Huddersfield and Sheffield Junction Railway (to a design by John Hawkshaw) carrying their railway south to Penistone along with their now closed branch to Holmfirth. The viaduct consists of 32 stone arches, the tallest of which is 121 feet in height. Each of the 32 arches is exactly 30 feet across, whereas the two larger skew arches on either end are 42 feet and 70 feet respectively.

The viaduct was built using local sandstone, which was quarried from the railway cutting at Berry Brow. The construction of the viaduct was a major undertaking, and at its peak, there were over 130 workers on site.

In 2009, the viaduct was the subject of a £3 million restoration project. The project included repairs to the stonework, the installation of new drainage, and the painting of the viaduct. The restoration project was completed in 2010 and the viaduct proudly carries the Penistone Line to this day.

One historical challenge regarding the viaduct is that of lobbing a cricket ball over the viaduct. The viaduct's height and width (136-foot (41 m) and 28 feet (8.5 m) respectively), means that the lob must be thrown to at least height of 180 feet (55 m) to succeed.

Some stories claim a train once arrived at

Huddersfield with a smashed window. Upon investigation a cricket ball was said to have been found in the carriage.

Jack Crum, a bowler with Armitage Bridge Cricket Club, was the first person confirmed to have thrown a ball over the viaduct, when on Saturday 10 September 1938, he succesfully completed the feat not once but twice in front of a crowd of around 60 onlookers.

Needless to say that this is one challenge that's best left to history, or at the very least the professional sports people, so please do NOT try this challenge yourself.

It is the largest stone railway viaduct in the United Kingdom and was the first viaduct in the world to be built using the "inverted arch" method.

The viaduct was built at a cost of £33,000, which, accounting for inflation would be around £3,000,000 in today's money.

LOCKWOOD

The current Lockwood station, which also opened in 1850, is a small, but well used, commuter station around a mile from Huddersfield where The Penistone Line terminates.

There's barely a hint left that it was once a major good station thanks to the neighbouring David Brown Engineering works. Founded in 1860, the company is one of the world's leading manufacturers of gears and gearboxes, and it was only as recently as the 1970s, with advances in trucks, that the large goods yard at the station was closed down.

From the station's opening it provided an important rail link for the community of Lockwood and was one of the many places where the infamous Lockwood Scar Ghost was spotted.

This terrifying ghost was said to be a man who had wild hair who would leap out at passersby, especially women and children, and would wave an umbrella angrily at those it encountered, before running away.

Some said it resembled a bear or even a gorilla.

According to contemporary reports, the ghost favoured dark places and would leap out when children or young women passed by, scaring them by wildly flailing its arms around.

It was spotted throughout March and April of 1862 and the town was in a frenzy wondering what strange forces were behind the odd encounters.

Police officers even witnessed the figure on multiple occasions and the newspapers of the era gave the entity the nickname of The Lockwood Scar Ghost, so called as he first appeared on a local road called Lockwood Scar, that led to Scar Mill.

This ghost would come to an end in the most unlikely of places: a courtroom.

A local man called Alfred Hanson, after a night's drinking at a local pub, saw the ghost and he wasn't afraid. He had a different reaction to everyone else, who had run in fear, for he punched the ghost in the head. The ghost, which felt like flesh and bone to Hanson, fell to the ground. In a moment of clarity Alfred realised that it wasn't a ghost at all. It was a man wearing some strange clothes and a man who had blackened up his face with soot.

Alfred kicked and beat the false spectre before himself running off into the night.

The following evening another man, Joshua Megson, stumbled across the ghost and he too opted to punch and beat the figure.

The following day a local barber called Matthew Shaw arrived at the local police station claiming to have been the victims of two separate, unprovoked, assaults. He clearly has been beaten, for he was battered and bruised, so the police took his statement and we're able to piece together what had happened.

Matthew Shaw? He was clearly The Lockwood Scar Ghost. The police then began to look into his life, to try and explain his odd behaviour, and found out that he was 58 and was recently widowed. Aside from that? He has good standing within the community.

They also quickly concluded that Shaw hadn't actually broken any laws. Wearing wild wigs, blackening one's face, waving an umbrella about, and pretending to be a gorilla weren't criminal offences at the time.

Because of this the matter was referred to the courts with both Hanson and Megson up on assault charges. The two men asked to be tried together, which was allowed, and called in over 60 defence witnesses who had all encountered the Lockwood Scar.

It was clear that, with the passing of his wife, something had snapped inside Matthew Shaw as the judge found his behaviour inexplicable. The assault charges against the two men were thrown out as the judge decided that Shaw had brought the beatings upon himself.

There were to be no more sightings of The Lockwood Scar ghost.

Because of this incident Shaw lost a lot of standing in the community and within 18 months he'd filed for bankruptcy. After that? He ended up in Crosland Moor Workhouse where he spent the rest of his life forced to work 12 hours a day. He eventually died, aged 76, in 1879.

HUDDERSFIELD

In the heart of West Yorkshire, Huddersfield Station stands as a testament to the region's rich industrial past. The station first opened its doors on August 1, 1847, as part of the Manchester and Leeds Railway. It served as a crucial transport hub, facilitating the movement of goods and people between these two major industrial cities.

Designed by architect James Pigott Pritchett, Huddersfield Station boasted an impressive

Victorian architectural style, characterised by its grand facade and intricate detailing. The station's construction was a testament to the flourishing textile industry in the region, which played a significant role in Huddersfield's prosperity during the 19th century.

Throughout its history, the station underwent several expansions and renovations to accommodate the growing demand for rail travel. The most significant development came in 1863 when a new, larger station building was constructed, designed by the renowned architect Charles Trubshaw. This expansion allowed for increased passenger capacity and improved facilities.

Huddersfield Station witnessed numerous milestones over the years. In 1920, it became a part of the London, Midland and Scottish Railway (LMS) network, following the amalgamation of several railway companies. The station continued to be a vital link in the rail network, serving as a gateway to the industrial heartland of West Yorkshire.

In the early 20th century, Huddersfield Station was a vital transportation hub, bustling with activity as workers and goods flowed through its platforms. Tragically, one dark afternoon in 1905, disaster struck. A devastating train collision occurred just outside the station, resulting in the loss of two lives and leaving dozens injured. A local service pulling into the station from Mirfield was hit by a mainline train that had been started in error. Extensive damage was done to both trains, and, in many ways, it's a miracle that only two people lost their lives. However, the echoes of that tragic night seem to reverberate within the station's walls to this day.

Over the years, station staff and late-night travellers have all reported eerie occurrences within Huddersfield Station. Footsteps echo down the platforms when no one is there, and cold drafts sweep through empty waiting areas. Some claim to have seen fleeting apparitions, dressed in old-fashioned clothing, as if frozen in time.

Some believe that the ghostly presence at Huddersfield Station is caused by the spirits of those who perished in the tragic 1905 train collision. It is said they remain tethered to the station, unable to move on, forever trapped in a spectral limbo. Whether they seek solace, redemption, or simply haunt the place where their lives met an untimely end, their presence serves as a poignant reminder of the price paid during the age of industrial progress.

So, if you find yourself waiting on a desolate platform at Huddersfield Station late at night, keep your senses alert. Listen for the echoes of distant voices, feel for an unexplained chill in the air, and maybe, just maybe, you might catch a glimpse of the ethereal figures that linger amidst the station's historic architecture.

The train crash of 1905 wasn't the only fatal accident at Huddersfield Station. Back in the 1870s, there was a surly porter at the station called Jonah. His dry, sarcastic sense of humour meant that people either loved him for his sardonic wit or, more often than not, they grew to loathe him. His laugh was said to be the sound of spite personified, as he revelled in laughing at others' misfortunes, sometimes intentionally sending passengers to the wrong platform, making them miss their trains, and then laughing in their faces if they had the temerity to dare complain.

In the late 1870s, however, the joke was on Jonah. Some locals, tired of his attitude, decided to play him at his own game, laughing with glee as he ran to the wrong platform to intercept an important mail train. Not wanting to be seen to be late, Jonah decided the best thing to do was to dart across the tracks, and was ironically hit by the very train he intended to intercept. Realising immediately that his working days were over, and thinking he might die as he'd just seen his own leg fly past his head, he shouted out to all present, promising to haunt the station from the great beyond and to make everyone's life a misery.

Jonah was seriously injured in the collision, ultimately losing his right leg, leaving him unable to work. However, his vow to haunt the station was largely forgotten. Jonah died in 1911, and on the day that he did, in fact on the very minute of his passing, his dark laughter reverberated around the station, coming from every direction all at once.

Ever since his death his laughter has, on occasion, returned to the station whenever there's a minor mishap.

So, if you've just heard an announcement at the station, saying that a train has been delayed or cancelled, listen very carefully as you might just be able to hear Old Jonah's laughter from the great beyond fulfilling his promise of haunting the station and revelling in the misery of others.

JACKPOT MARY

The former bingo hall in Huddersfield is said to be haunted by the ghost of a woman who won the jackpot, only to collapse with a heart attack caused by the shock. She later died in hospital.

The woman's name was Mary, and she was a regular at the bingo hall. She was always hoping to win the jackpot, but she never seemed to be lucky.

One night, Mary was playing bingo as usual. She had been playing for hours, and she was starting to lose hope. But then, her number came up. She had won the jackpot!

Mary was so excited that she started to cry. She couldn't believe that she had finally won. But her excitement was short-lived. She collapsed with a heart attack, and she died in hospital a few days later.

Since then, Mary's ghost has been seen at the bingo hall. Since Mary's passing, she has been seen sitting in what would have been her favourite seat at the bingo hall or standing holding her winning bingo card.

Some people believe that Mary's ghost is still trying to come to terms with her death. They say that she is still trying to understand why she died, and why she died so suddenly. Others believe that she is simply trying to spread her luck to others. They say that she is trying to help other people win the jackpot, just like she did. Those who have sighted Mary are said to be more likely to win prizes.

A security guard was patrolling the hall one night several years after it had closed down. The owners were redeveloping the building and had issues with vandalism and theft. It was around 10pm when he saw Mary's ghost standing in the middle of the hall before it promptly vanished. The guard was so scared, not knowing the story of Mary and believing that it was kids playing a prank on him, that he called the police. They came out but nothing was found to be out of place.

The Bingo Hall has now been redeveloped and it is now Palace Studios halls of residence and Jackpot Mary is still said to haunt the area to this day.

Unlike many other ghosts, an encounter with her is said to be lucky, and to spark joy in those who see her.

THE HEALING GHOST

The small town of Meltham, near Huddersfield, is home to a number of ghost stories. One of the most well-known is the story of Annie, the ghost of a young girl who is said to haunt a council house in the town.

The story of Annie begins in 1961, when a family moved into the council house. The family consisted of a husband, wife, and their young son, who was suffering from meningitis. The son's condition was so severe that he was confined to bed, and his legs were paralyzed.

One night, the family was awakened by a loud noise coming from the son's bedroom. When they went to investigate, they saw a large, white entity sitting by the boy's bed. The entity was stroking the boy's legs, and the boy seemed to be comforted by its presence.

The family was terrified by the entity, but they also felt a sense of peace. They knew that the entity was trying to help their son, and they were grateful for its presence.

The next day, the family called a medium to come and investigate. The medium told them that the entity was the ghost of a young girl named Annie, from Huddersfield, who had died a few years earlier. Annie had also suffered from meningitis, and she had died from the disease.

The medium said that Annie was trying to help the boy because she knew what he was going through. She was also trying to give the family comfort in their time of need.

The family was relieved to hear this, and they were grateful to Annie for her help. Over the next few weeks, the figure continued to visit their son, and his condition gradually improved.

After a couple of years, the son regained the use of his legs, and the figure never appeared again. The family believes that Annie had helped their son to heal, and they are grateful for her kindness.

The family continued to live in the council house for many years, and they never experienced any more paranormal activity. However, they never forgot the kindness of Annie, the ghost who helped their son to heal.

GHOSTS ON THE LINES

In our final chapter I am going to share a few stories taken from the other Strange Britain books, showing that rather than be confined to The Penistone Line, ghostly encounters happen all across the rail network.

The final story is one from personal experience.

The Ghost Train Of Fairfield Station

Fairfield Station, to the east of Manchester, is a quiet little suburban station. It is, in a word, basic.

It now has just two platforms and a couple of simple wooden shelters. However, it wasn't always this way. Before 1958, it was considered a busy and bustling station with six platforms. The Beeching cuts of the 1960s stripped the station right back.

But ever since those cuts, the station has still had an occasional visitor from the era of steam.

On certain nights around sunset, when autumn is

turning to winter, an old green steam locomotive can sometimes be seen chugging its way along the tracks, pulling along a couple of coaches.

If you're on the platforms, it is said that you can often hear its distinctive whistle, although the train itself has never been seen from platform level. However, if you're on Booth Road on the bridge over the station and happen to be looking down towards the platforms, you might just get a glimpse, as that's where all the sightings have been made.

The train steams in from the east, running along what were the old express tracks, before promptly vanishing under the bridge.

Perhaps it's heading to the site of the nearby Gorton Tank, which opened in 1847 and was a huge factory specialising in the production of steam trains. By the late 1950s, thanks to the rise of diesel and electric trains, it was being used as a decommissioning plant for the old steam stock before finally closing its doors in 1963.

If you're feeling brave in late November, head on up to the bridge on Booth Road and have a look down towards the station. If you're lucky, you too might see the phantom green train passing by below.

Mayfield Station

Manchester's Mayfield Station was opened in 1910 to provide relief to the London Road Station, which was suffering from serious overcrowding.

From very early in the station's history, it gained the unsavoury reputation of being a suicide hotspot. People would either leap in front of trains or, more often than not, attempt to jump from the station's high roof. A survivor of such an attempt said it felt as though a dark and unseen force had "taken over" their body and that they were just a "passenger." They were fully aware of what their body was planning, and were screaming inside to try and prevent it, but they were powerless to do anything other than watch.

It reached the point where passengers would actively avoid the station if at all possible.

In 1960, this decline in footfall led to the station's closure. Instead of a passenger station, it became a hub for Royal Mail trains as well as a major sorting office. In the same year, the neighbouring Manchester London Road Station was renamed to Manchester Piccadilly, the name it still holds to this day.

Throughout its later life as a Royal Mail depot, there were parts of the former station that were deliberately avoided. No one could fully articulate why, other than that those parts of the station just "felt wrong."

In 1986, Royal Mail closed the site down. Trucks had made the need for a dedicated post station obsolete, and ever since then it has been left largely to fall into disrepair.

There have been countless plans to regenerate the area, as it is a huge chunk of unused and therefore valuable land in Central Manchester. As of this writing, its destruction is planned to make way for a combined business and leisure complex.

However, when it comes to the old Mayfield Station, the same plans have been submitted off and on since the 1980s, and for one reason or another, they have never come to fruition.

It is almost as if people know, on some primitive instinctual level, that there is a dark force lurking there, and they know to avoid it at all costs.

The Ghost Train Of Mapperley Tunnel

Although it is hard to believe today, the north of Nottingham was once criss-crossed by several railway lines.

Mapperley Tunnel was built as part of the Great Northern Railway's extension line that ran from Colwick Junction all the way to Egginton Junction near Burton on Trent.

The tunnel was about two-thirds of a mile long and opened originally in 1875. In 1925, it suffered a partial collapse due to the mine shafts of Gedling Colliery being dug directly underneath it.

Despite the initial collapse being repaired, the tunnel suffered further damage as a result of the colliery, which led to its eventual closure in 1960.

The western end of the tunnel totally collapsed, but the cutting that ran down to it is behind the Scout Hut at Woodthorpe. The eastern end of the tunnel is still open, but is on private land, near Arnold Lane and Gedling Country Park. If you have permission from the landowner, you can make it about halfway down the tunnel before a massive pile of rubbish blocks your way. If you could clear the rubbish mountain, you would find that the rest of the tunnel has totally collapsed. Train enthusiasts and urban explorers have dubbed the rubbish mountain the "Mapperley Stack."

Back in the late 1970s, a group of kids were playing in the tunnel having gotten in from the eastern end. It was then that they heard a steam train in the distance and it sounded like it was getting closer and closer. The kids ran for their lives, charging out of the tunnel, all the while fully expecting to be hit by a speeding train. When they emerged into daylight, rational thought returned to them and they realised that there couldn't have been a train in the tunnel.

The other end was blocked. They must have heard a ghost train!

It's not just within the tunnel itself that the ghost train has been heard steaming along. Houses around the collapsed eastern end, both in Woodthorpe and as far away as Plains Estate, have also heard the distinctive sound of a steam train hurtling by. But as anyone in that part of Nottingham knows, it's currently a good few miles from the closest surviving railway line.

This is one ghost train that I myself have heard.

It was in April 2014 and my partner woke up claiming she'd heard a steam train the night before. I'd heard the stories, and I'd experienced strange things, but I just laughed it off. We were miles and miles from the nearest train line, I assured her, before going back to sleep. Then the next night we were laying in bed when we both went quiet as we heard it. From the sounds, it was a train composed of quite a few carriages and it sounded to be in a hurry.

Perhaps this is the stone tape theory at play? Somehow the area has retained the memory of the many trains that once regularly sped along the line. And every now and again, the sounds, by means unknown, are once again brought to life in the form of an invisible ghost train passing along its old route.

SPECIAL THANKS TO THE PENISTONE LINE PARTNERSHIP

The Penistone Line Partnership (PLP) is a community rail partnership that was formed in 1993 to promote and encourage the use of the line. It was the first community rail partnership in the UK, and it has been credited with helping to save the Penistone Line from closure.

In the early 1980s, the line was threatened with closure due to low passenger numbers. However, a campaign led by the Penistone Line Users' Association and the PLP was successful in persuading British Rail to keep the line open.

Since then, the PLP has worked to improve the service on the Penistone Line and to promote its use. As a result of the PLP's work, passenger numbers on the Penistone Line have more than doubled since 1993. The line now carries over a million passengers a year, and it is considered to be an important economic and social asset for the local area.

The PLP is a not-for-profit organisation that is funded by a combination of grants, donations, and membership fees. The partnership is governed by a board of directors, which is made up of representatives from local businesses, community groups, and the rail industry.

The PLP is committed to working with its partners to ensure that the Penistone Line continues to provide a vital transport link for the local area. The partnership is also committed to promoting the line as a tourist destination, and it is working to develop new walking and cycling trails along the line.

The PLP also hosts various special events along the line. They have had real ale trains, jazz trains, acoustic music trains, and even a ghost train.

Their website is:

https://penline.co.uk

If you're in Sheffield why not join Adrian Finney on one of his **Strange Sheffield Ghost Walks**? Full details can be found at:

https://strangebritain.eventbrite.com

Darkest Night tells the story of the city's darkest night, during World War II, as well as the city's connection to a fabled character from English Folklore.

Plague Pits to Paradise includes an unlikely Victorian Ghost as well as tales of a former mortuary, a pub with a poltergeist, and a haunted theatre.

The Infamous Bunting Nook takes the brave along one of England's most haunted roads to hear tales of headless horseman and demonic black dogs.

Plus there are regular specials, including True Crime nights, throughout the year.

Printed in Great Britain
by Amazon